This charming book gave me tw… which necessarily must ex… with making a strong … the case for optir… that we are helples… …ns – but we can do far mor…

– Rory Sutherland, deput… …y

If there was ever a time to be a better human, it might just be now. My heart was tickled, my soul was touched and my brain was provoked into action by Mike Dickson's simple but smart book that charmingly yet cogently lays out the case for kindness. We all know it but do we know how to act it? Mike's book offers tales, tools and tempting bite-sized bits of advice for all of us to act. No matter who we are, we can all be kinder – and in so doing, we might just change the world.

– Lucy Cleland, editor/co-founder, *Country & Town House* magazine

That first moment of serendipity which led Mike to found Whizz-Kidz completely transformed so many lives, including mine. One act started a 'kindness chain', resulting in countless smiles and freedom for so many disabled young people and their families. This book in itself is an act of kindness – it is an inspiring reminder that with a little awareness, love, kindness and a desire to help, you CAN change the world, or simply make someone's day a better one.

– Arumina Misra, lawyer; Whizz-Kidz trustee; director, Wheelchair Alliance

This book could be the seed of the counter movement we so badly need in this moment: in the face of fear, anger and hatred, it makes a compelling case that being human starts and ends with love. The kind of help it advocates is about coming alongside one another and asking what it is we can do to support, connect and set each other free to live our fullest lives. Profound and essential, from one who truly practises what he preaches.

– Jon Alexander, author of *Citizens*

First Edition

HOW TO BE A BETTER HUMAN

Mike Dickson

BB

London, United Kingdom

Byline Books
London, United Kingdom

First published in the United Kingdom of Great Britain and Northern Ireland by Byline Books, 2025

Cover Design by Mecob

Layout by Prepare to Publish
Printed in Great Britain by TJ Books

ISBN UK: 978-1-916754-15-7

For Shuna, Annabel and Will.
My three best friends, who have
given me so much.

Luke

Contents

The more you give, the more you get
The more you laugh, the less you fret. The
more you do unselfishly,
The more you live abundantly.
The more of everything you share,
The more you'll always have to spare
The more you love, the more you'll find That
life is good and friends are kind.
For only what we give away,
Enriches us from day to day.

Helen Steiner Rice

Foreword

By Tim Smit
Founder, the Eden Project

Oscar Wilde once said, "No one remembers the well-mannered person at the party." His point? Life's too short to go through it quietly. If you've shown up, don't just sit in the corner. Participate. Connect. Make it count.

Some years ago, I was asked to speak at a leadership event for a room full of financial services professionals. At the end of the talk, a young man asked, "What's the biggest mistake you've ever made?"

I didn't hesitate. "I've made two great mistakes in my life," I said. "And neither had anything to do with business."

The first was this: not visiting older relatives and friends when they invited me. I was busy, chasing my career. And then they were gone. The guilt of that – of the blind selfishness that led me to disappoint people who had looked out for me – stays with you. You carry it, gently but persistently, for the rest of your life.

The second came in response to a different question: "What's the most important book you've ever read?"

My answer? *Mrs Beeton's Book of Household Management.*

That got a good laugh. People thought I was joking and were waiting for the punchline. But I was being deadly serious.

While researching traditional fruit and veg for a book I was writing, I found myself leafing through *Mrs Beeton*, and stumbled on a chapter titled 'On Ladies' Deportment'. I kept reading – I've no idea why – and it changed my life. Mrs Beeton suggested that when a young woman was first introduced to Society, she should carry a small pencil and notebook in her stocking. That way, if someone mentioned, say, Miss Ross performing splendidly in Mr Sheridan's play at the theatre, she could later jot down the reference and, over time, collect stories and insights to join future conversations.

It hit me like a thunderbolt. I'd spent decades dismissing small talk as trivial. But in that moment, I realised my mistake: small talk is the biggest talk of all.

It's not about the weather. It's an opening gambit. An act of hope. A nervous "hello" or "might rain later" is often code for something much deeper: I don't know how to start this. I want to belong. I want to connect. Please meet me halfway.

Now tell me that's not the most human thing of all.

This book is full of such realisations. It's a gentle, powerful nudge from someone who's walked the path and wants to help you find yours. Mike's stories are generous and quietly profound. They ask us to show up for our friends, our families, our communities and, most of all, for ourselves.

I'm writing this before I head to my happy place for a family holiday. I'm thinking of the people I love, the lives we build through countless tiny interactions, and of something my grandmother said before she died: "Make sure that when your time comes, you say 'I'm glad I did' not 'I wish I had'."

This book is a heartfelt antidote to that second sentence. Be glad you did!

Read it with a smile on your face, love in your heart, and a promise to act on what it stirs in you. There's great wisdom here if you're ready for it. Enjoy.

Introduction

I often muttered to myself that if I ever wrote a book I'd call it *Surprised by Life*, because I'm quite frankly a bit stunned at how my life has turned out. It's totally changed direction from a determination in my twenties to be successful (whatever I had in mind that definitely involved lots of money) to the far happier life I live today. So this short book is to share what I've learnt, because I promise you the sooner you start that journey toward genuine fulfilment, the more fun you'll have.

I had a less than idyllic childhood, never really understood what was going on at school and left at 17, determined to make a fortune. I didn't but I did create a small, successful bicycle sales and rental business (years ahead of its time!).

But on the journey my priorities, and the lens through which I looked at the world, changed.

One day I was challenged to run the London Marathon. I agreed to do it and invited another mad friend, Ricky, to join me. Mad because neither of us had run more than to catch a bus for years.

In simple terms we decided we were going to run 26.2 miles to fund a powered wheelchair for Sammy, a young girl with cerebral palsy who couldn't move, so she could get about independently.

We both 'got round' and raised more than enough for Sammy's wheelchair. That story is in the next chapter.

For now, I want to focus on what I like to think of as moments of serendipity. This was several, one after the other, and gave birth to Whizz-Kidz,[1] a charity which over the last 35 years has become the largest supplier of paediatric mobility aids outside the NHS, and has changed thousands of children's lives.

1 Whizz Kidz: whizz-kidz.org.uk

More than that, it was the start of my journey over the years supporting amazing individuals with a passion to create positive change and connecting them with others who can support and help them grow.

I have learned what many of you likely already know to be true: That helping others gives you a genuine sense of satisfaction and a quiet purpose.

In these dark and dangerous times, when the world nationally and internationally is full of challenges, and the daily news is relentlessly grim, it is so easy to be overwhelmed. But this is our time to step up, come alongside and care for each other – our family, friends, colleagues at work, people we know, other people we don't know and make a difference to their lives.

With a little love and care.

Because it matters and because we can, despite

the fact it's easy to feel overwhelmed by the news on a daily basis.

I find it impossible to ignore the war between Russia and Ukraine; the deaths of tens of thousands of innocent people including so many children in Gaza, in the tinder box that is the Middle East; the forgotten war in Sudan, the desperate plight of one million-plus Rohingya refugees who fled Myanmar and are now living in camps in Bangladesh;[2] the shocking inability of the world's governments to tackle the climate crisis properly after *thirty years* of COP conferences.

2 www.unrefugees.org/news/rohingya-refugees-crisis-explained

In the UK, 14.3 million people experience levels of poverty and hunger so extreme they rely on charity food handouts.

And 4.5 million children are living in poverty – that's 3 in every 10, or put another way, almost a third in every classroom.[3]

3 Living in poverty: www.actionforchildren.org.uk/blog/where-is-child-poverty-increasing-in-the-uk

A poll by the Mental Health Foundation in 2023 found 73% of UK adults saying they had felt anxious in the previous two weeks, with 26% saying it prevented them from doing what they wanted to do.[4] The time it takes to get treatment with our much-loved NHS; the shameful pollution of our coasts, rivers and lakes by the water companies; the relentless stream of bad news from the media... It's constant and, at times, overwhelming.

4 Mental health: www.mentalhealth.org.uk/our-work/public-engagement/mental-health-awareness-week/anxiety-report

It's natural to care about others, and the natural world, and the people suffering and dying in war zones and disaster areas. We want to live in a better world, or at least improve our own part of it.

We just need to clearly understand that every single one of us is facing personal challenges. We can resolve some of the problems in our own lives and the lives of others by listening, coming alongside each other and actively helping. And we can support those doing the helping by exercising our own people skills and leading with our humanity and our hearts.

There is enormous power in small actions.

I hope when you read some of the stories in this book about people who've created change simply and without fuss, you'll feel inspired to pause and think about what you can do. This isn't about how 'someone else' needs to fix things, but how *you* can shift the dial, simply by pausing, listening and working out how you can turn up for one another with a little love and care. And the wonderful thing is you'll feel much better about life when you do.

“If you only do one thing today, show up and let someone know they’re loved”

John Sweeney, co-founder of Drop Dead Generous and the kindest man I know.

1.

A simple 'yes' that changed my life

I was 41 years old and at a Christmas party. Our host worked for one of the London Marathon sponsors and had a handful of free entries, so who was up for running?

Feeling very much at peace with the world after several glasses of wine, I put my hand up and said yes. Then I went home and forgot all about it.

On 18 January – a day ingrained in my brain forever – a helpful fax arrived at work (yes, it was that long ago) with a note: "You have twelve weeks till the London Marathon, here is a get-you-round-in-one-piece schedule."

Slightly shocked, I went home, and that night over supper with friends as I waved the fax in one hand and a large gin and tonic in the other, one of them offered to donate £1,000 to a charity of my choice if I did it.

My bluff had been called. I had never intentionally run anywhere since school. I started training – slowly

– and called an equally non-athletic friend, Ricky, inviting him to join me in my latest adventure.

The weeks passed. As race day drew closer I decided that if I was going to go through all the pain and suffering I might as well do it for something worthwhile. It's amazing how serendipity works.

Months before, a young girl in a powered wheelchair had driven into the bicycle shop I owned in Covent Garden. She pressed a control that raised her seat until she was the same height as the counter, bought an item, lowered the seat, then sped out into the piazza. I had been intrigued enough to remember the name of the manufacturers and called them to discover that each wheelchair cost £3,500 and there was a waiting list of 120.

Was there someone really deserving we could raise money for? They suggested a young girl called Sammy, who had cerebral palsy and lived in Lincoln. As much to give myself courage and inspiration for the marathon ahead as anything else, I cleared a day from my diary and got on a train.

Sammy and her grandmother met me and took me home to tea. I had never met a disabled child and had no idea what cerebral palsy was. I spent about two hours with them and was profoundly moved. Sammy was very bright but had great trouble with her speech and her heavy wheelchair meant she was unable to move around at all without being pushed. I asked Sammy for a photo I could use to share her story and returned to London to report back to Ricky. We agreed to fundraise to buy Sammy her powered wheelchair then sent letters to all our friends with her photo and the message: "We are going to do something daft and mildly heroic; run 26.2 miles to raise money to help a young girl who can't move to become independently mobile, get around in her own home, 'whizz' about and go shopping, get around at school, play with friends, take part in sport."

By the day of the London Marathon in 1989 neither of us had run more than six miles, but we had raised over £9,000, an extraordinary sum in those days. Some people even sponsored us to cross the starting line! We hugged each other, exclaimed "All for one and one for all" and set off into the unknown, with almost no idea of what we were doing. Six hours and thirty minutes later, when all the traffic separation schemes had been removed, I staggered across the finishing line! Ricky had made it in a more respectable five hours. Mission accomplished. We headed home for a hot bath and then a great celebratory dinner with our wives, overjoyed, exhausted and proudly wearing our medals.

When we went to the factory where Sammy's wheelchair was made, we were able to be there the moment she first sat in it. She learned to move it about in minutes. Suddenly, she could whizz about on her own. It was a very special moment. We sent a picture of a very happy Sammy, sitting in her brand-new powered wheelchair, to everyone who had sponsored us and of course their feedback was wonderful. We were truthfully both surprised and very moved by their reactions.

As the money came in, questions were asked: "There must be lots of children like Sammy needing wheelchairs. Are there charities to help them?" Ricky (another moment of serendipity) was a senior paediatrician at Great Ormond Street Hospital and arranged a meeting with the major disability charities – we didn't want to duplicate and knew nothing about the charity world – and the response was 100% positive. No one was doing this. We had identified a genuine need. Out of the blue came even more serendipity. A friend with charity experience offered to help register a charity; another offered seed funding to help us get started. Shuna, my wife, offered us a desk and a phone line in her office.

Six months later nine of us ran the New York Marathon, raising £45,000. In April 1990, just a year after Ricky and I had made it round London, he, Shuna and I registered Whizz-Kidz as a charity.

Never in my wildest dreams did I think of the impact getting round a marathon slowly would have. Together with Ricky and Shuna I became a co-founder, later CEO, of one of the fastest-growing charities in the UK. Since 1990 Whizz-Kidz has raised over £150 million, provided wheelchairs and equipment for more than 26,000 young people and directly supported young wheelchair users to greater independence more than 48,000 times.

The improvement in mobility helped to make

Sammy's life a little better – and it completely changed mine. I gradually awakened from my own small, self-obsessed world. I discovered how charities work, and I began to learn first hand about the impact and rewards of giving. I realised that when people go out of their way to help others, at any level, they often get back as much, or more, than they give. I noticed that when Whizz-Kidz fundraisers met a disabled young person, often the child for whom they had raised money, the impact on them was enormous. They were both moved and humbled that their efforts had helped a child who was unable to move, move. "The best thing I have done all year," they said again and again.

I, too, was amazed and humbled. By the optimism and spirit of the disabled children I met and by the amazing families who looked after them with such astonishing patience and love. By the care and attention of those surrounding the children – the carers and physiotherapists, the occupational therapists, the manufacturers of the special mobility equipment.

It was wonderful to watch and to be involved in, albeit in a very small way. I discovered what an enormous privilege it is to be able to help others and how hugely rewarding it is to be able to inspire all kinds of other people to do so.

I also learned that being curious, personally taking the time to find out what was going on, engaging in a genuine real-life experience and going beyond my own boundaries was the best way possible to learn, rather than 'just searching the web'.

I was 41 and it had taken me that long to discover my real purpose. To inspire and encourage people to help others.

Imagine the amazing impact everyone could make if they started younger than me. Anyone can change their world for the better when you listen carefully and follow your heart. It doesn't require money. When you think about it, all I did was say "yes".

We may not realise it at the time but there is a wonderful 'ripple effect' that begins with a life of its own when we take small actions. Helen Steiner Rice's poem is spot on. The more you give, the more you'll be rewarded in ways that will change your life for the better. Why not start today?

2.

Now's the time to show up

> "Be kind. For everyone you meet is fighting a hard battle"
>
> Rev John Watson, 1897

I agree with Watson. We're all insecure. And anxious. Including me – obviously. We wouldn't be human if we didn't worry about our relationships, our families, our work, our finances, our health and more. Not all of them all the time, but definitely some of them much of the time. And every single one of us, every person you know, has their down days or periods when they struggle, lose their bounce and become depressed.

We are all vulnerable and we all need help from other people. Just in case you think this isn't true, take a few minutes right now to think of your three closest friends – people you know really well.

Write their names down and think about each one of them for a moment. How are they?

Outwardly they may seem not to have a care in the world, but I'd like to suggest to you that each of them is worried about something important that's impacting their lives. What is it?

It naturally follows that if they are, so is everyone else you know. Yes – everyone. All your friends, the members of your family, everyone at work, in your local community, at every party you go to, in each pub, bar, café, restaurant you visit... I am sure you get my point.

Time to show up. To think about the people who

live in these different areas of your life and how you can help them. And other people outside your normal world, those you don't know at all and who you would never normally notice.

Simply, practically, thoughtfully and with care and a little love. My message is that you don't need to be powerful or wealthy to make a difference. Everyone has that superpower. You can't, and shouldn't, expect something in return for these actions; just trust your instinct and see where it leads you and remember to tread carefully with one another.

This is not a 'self-help book' – though hopefully after reading you will feel much better about your own life. It is a 'help-others book'. Because you are fortunate, because you can and because helping others matters.

I could add some statistics, charts and graphs here to illustrate this but, honestly, you know it is true. Think of the last time someone did something to help you and how surprised and grateful you were. How did you feel?

Research by the charity Action for Happiness has identified 10 'Keys to Happier Living'.[5] As they say, everyone's different, but happiness grows when you trust that others are there for you. And others need to feel listened to and understood. Refocusing our brains and thoughts away from 'what's wrong' to noticing 'what's right' works. It's that simple.

5 Action for Happiness: actionforhappiness.org

Action for Happiness's 10 Keys to Happier Living

If you're still not sure, Harvard University, no less, has *eighty-five* years of research into what makes people happy. Surely being happy must be linked to wealth, health and success? Not so. If you wish to live a happier life, just spend more time nurturing others and yourself through positive relationships.[6] They will keep us happier, healthier and help us live longer. Period.

Still need convincing? Goldman Sachs is a global leader in investment banking, with clients who we'd all probably agree are rich. So it's interesting that their own consumer research found that only 1% of those surveyed rated 'being rich' as an important part of their self-worth.[7]

What are you waiting for?

6 Harvard research on the secret to a happy life: www.cnbc.com/2023/02/10/85-year-harvard-study-found-the-secret-to-a-long-happy-and-successful-life.html

7 Goldman Sachs research on what rich people value most: www.marcus.co.uk/content/dam/mosaic/shared/img/news-and-insight/worth/An_Exploration_of_Worth_Marcus_by_Goldman_Sachs.pdf

Ubuntu: the essence of being human

I was lucky enough to meet Archbishop Desmond Tutu in person and get to know him a little. The experience of following him into a hotel in Cape Town has stayed with me. Not only did he know the porters, receptionists and waiters by name, he knew them well enough to enquire about their wives and children – also by name. He was on his way to a public lunch, but not too busy to pause and speak to everyone and not pass them by.

As he explained to me, it is just part of *ubuntu*:

"In our African culture, there is something very difficult to put into English – 'ubuntu'. Ubuntu speaks about the essence of being human. We say that a person is a person through other persons... that it is impossible to be human as a solitary individual... that we are created for inter-dependence, and my humanity is caught up in your humanity. I need you to be all you can be in order for me to become all I can be. Forgiveness is therefore not altruistic but is instead the best form of self-interest. Conversely, a person who dehumanises another is also dehumanised."

"It is one of the beautiful compensations of life that no man can sincerely try to help another without helping himself."

Ralph Waldo Emerson

3.
What is the point of you?

> "Tell me, what is it you plan to do with your one wild and precious life?"
>
> Mary Oliver (1935–2019), American poet

I'm always grateful that I started becoming useful, knowing that I had found what to do with my "one wild and precious life" – albeit gradually and accidentally – in my 40s. (And I'm still trying to live up to that thought!)

If you're still wondering what you are here for, perhaps now's the time to have a word with yourself about this one big adventure we have called 'life'. What are the really important things that matter to you?

When I was at school – several hundred years ago – studying Shakespeare was mandatory for my equivalent of GCSE English, with the result of putting me off him for ages. That was until I began going to see his plays on stage and in films and realised he was a brilliant communicator – even a genius – in writing about every human emotion and condition with astonishing perception. I'm sure you'll recognise many lines – "To be or not to be" from *Hamlet* or "If music be the food of love, play on" from *Twelfth Night* – even if you can't recite them verbatim. Shakespeare's wisdom from four hundred years ago is still totally relevant today.

The speech I'd like you to think about right now is one of the best known and most quoted from *As You Like It*, published in 1623:

> "All the world's a stage,
> And all the men and women merely players;
> They have their exits and their entrances,
> And one man in his time plays many parts,
> His acts being seven ages..."

From infant to "whining schoolboy" to the final, seventh age and last scene of all:

> "That ends this strange eventful history,
> Is second childishness and mere oblivion;
> Sans teeth, sans eyes, sans taste, sans
> everything."

Life expectancy is greater now, around 80 years, and of course often much longer for many. But in the grand scheme of things our lives are very short. To put them in perspective, an article in American news outlet the *Huffington Post* broke it down as follows:

Over 80 years we will spend approximately:

- 26 years asleep, plus 7 trying to get to sleep – a total of 33 years
- 13 years at work – that's 26% of a typical working period of 50 years
- 11 years watching screens (Netflix, streaming, catching up on social media...)
- 4½ years eating
- 3 years on holiday
- 1.4 years exercising.[8]

Added up, that's around 66 years doing what we do, before adding in another eight years for education, romance, meeting real people in person, queuing – even housework.

This leaves roughly only six years of unallocated 'free' life left, which you may find slightly depressing. On the other hand it might spur you into action and encourage you to ask yourself if you are making the best of the only life you have. Think about this for a while.

If you're reading this in your late 30s or early 40s, you probably have three or four years of unallocated time left to be useful. Provided, of course, you don't become ill, end up in a car crash or something else you've never dreamed of comes at you out of the blue and you say goodbye to life a little earlier.

Or, if you're in your late teens or twenties, evidence suggests that more of you will live longer – many to over 100! So you have a wonderful opportunity to

8 Huffington Post on how we spend our years: www.huffingtonpost.co.uk/entry/weve-broken-down-your-entire-life-into-years-spent-doing tasks_n_61087617e4b0999d2084fec5

create a life that is both enjoyable and fruitful from the get-go. You may even have a full decade of this so-called unallocated life left.

So how *are* you going to spend the rest of your 'free time'? What is going to be your contribution?

Wonderfully, in every area of life, people become very good at what they do: in the academic world, medicine, fire fighters, social workers, dustmen, street cleaners, charity workers, taxi drivers, vicars, gardeners, builders, fishermen, farmers, retailers, journalists, writers and every other 'job' out there – if I haven't mentioned your world, please forgive me. People work hard, succeed at many different levels and are usually rewarded in a suitable fashion. Or paid the rate, often not nearly enough, for the job.

You may be one of the millions of people in the UK and the world who care for others with dementia, cancer, mental health challenges, Parkinson's, a disability and so on, helping people without food or homes, trapped in poverty... or just being a very kind neighbour.

It seems blindingly obvious that if we all looked out for each other in our own communities there'd be much less loneliness, anxiety and depression, because we know they're linked. It just needs more of us to proactively care.

It's time to engage your gentle, caring side. To show kindness, thoughtfulness and empathy, the best part of you, the real you that spends too much time buried beneath the hustle, stress and problems of everyday life. The part that is moved by music, cries during soppy films, loves good friends and is touched by the plights of others, in this country and around the world.

I agree with the purpose of life Stephen Covey and Roger Merrill identified In their book *First Things First* – to live, to love, to learn and to leave a legacy.[9] Summing it up:

9 Stephen R. Covey & A. Roger Merrill, *First Things First*, 1999.

- **To live** – as in Maslow's hierarchy of needs – is to find shelter, food, clothing and a good way to earn a living.
- **To love** is to recognise our need to love and to be loved.
- **To learn** is to develop and grow mentally to become a little bit wiser all the time.
- **To leave a legacy** is to feel that we have all left this world a little better for having been here. This speaks to our spiritual need for a sense of purpose, personal consequence and contribution.

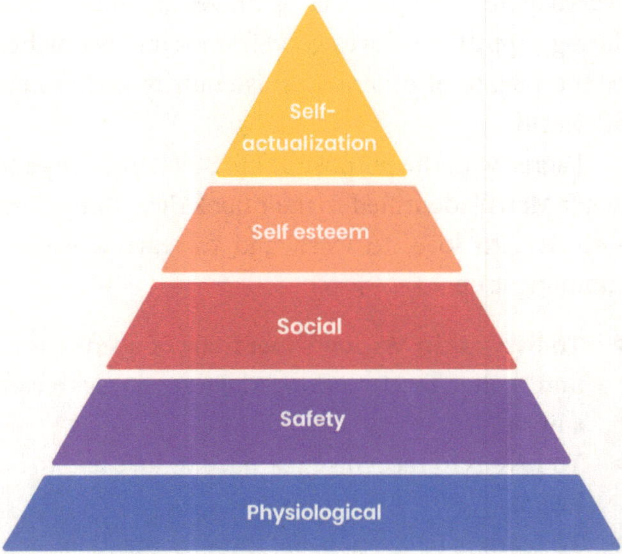

Maslow's hierarchy of needs

You have to be able to earn a living, afford somewhere to live and be able to buy food. But if that is covered, you only have to remember two things to be happier:

1. Giving your love to others and being loved, because it's part of our DNA. Very few of us thrive alone.
2. Your legacy. "Why am I here? What memories will be held onto after I've gone?" In Ken Robinson's simple terms, "What you do for yourself dies with you. What you do for others lives on." Your contribution to the lives of others matters if you want to leave a trace on humanity, however small.

You will be happier, live longer and thrive best when you have friends you love because it is likely through these relationships you will discover a life that's both 'wild and precious', filled with happy memories and laughter.

Mac's three questions

Mac Macartney is an inspirational speaker, writer and lover "of all things in life... attempting to build bridges that connect like and unlike minds and hearts".[10] He encourages everyone to ask themselves three questions:

1. What is it that you most deeply and profoundly love?
2. What are your deepest and most profound gifts?
3. What are my deepest and most profound responsibilities?

10 Mac Macartney: macmacartney.com. His book: *The Children's Fire: Heart Song of a People*, 2018

I need to mention money here. Anyone living with debt and being stretched to pay for basic heating and food knows money is important and lack of it hugely stressful. But if you are managing and have a bit saved for emergencies, how much more do you need to make you happy? Don't believe that a yacht, amazing holiday or more stuff will make you happier, as over and over again the evidence shows it won't.

It's just about thinking about others and their

needs and finding ways to make space to come alongside them and find out how they are. We need to pause, peek out from our own enormously busy, important, stressful lives and pay attention to others – their challenges and problems. To care about each other.

Today – and every day.

As the great poet William Wordsworth wrote

"...that best portion of a good man's life,
His little, nameless, unremembered acts
Of kindness and of love..."

Wisdom from *The Children's Fire*: A story from Mac Macartney

The Children's Fire is a story, a symbol, a fragment of ancient wisdom, a longing and a way of thinking and perceiving from the indigenous peoples of North America.

A few hundred years ago, wise elders of a people who over a few short decades would see their former way of life disappear forever enquired deeply into questions concerning life, living, dying, relationship and meaning and the question, "How shall we serve the best interests of our people?"

One of the great challenges the elders

considered was the complex relationship between the short and long term. Almost always leaders that started out with the best intentions over time started to serve the best interests of themselves rather than the people.

The Children's Fire was lit as a living symbol and the chiefs sat and deliberated around it. They understood that their children, and beyond them all living things, were the tribe's future. The solemn pledge they made to the fire was that:

No law, no decision, no action, nothing of any kind will be permitted to go out from this council of chiefs that will harm the children.

Only when each had made that pledge were they allowed to take their seat on the council of leaders.

The Children's Fire is a regenerative principle, a lodestar guiding the deliberations of leaders who are charged with the responsibility of governance and the long-term welfare of their people – the same meaning we ascribe to the concept of sustainability. It's a pledge to life, a commitment to the responsibility carried by each successive generation to safeguard the vitality and regenerative capacity of the Earth.

The Children's Fire is a simple and wonderful vision that our human purpose is to care for all things. It's very pragmatic. It doesn't require you to believe in anything, just acknowledge the wisdom it speaks of and apply the principle in action. It could be a pivot point to redesign our society so that every child emerges from education feeling good about who they are. Every farmer, every politician, every new business is committed to joining that circle. Everyone can be invited to join. We are all chiefs.

4. Your family

"A group of people who are related to each other, such as a mother, a father, and their children"

The Cambridge Dictionary

"A family is not a group of people who share blood, but those who share a story."

Gabriel Garcia Marquez

Many families are happy, grow together, celebrate birthdays, marriages and the birth of children, and support each other throughout their lives. If you're lucky enough to have a great family, this is a call to constantly nurture those closest to you as no relationships will last longer. If you weren't blessed with a loving and supportive family, you can build your own.

The family unit of mum, dad and kids is now in the

minority. Forty-two per cent of UK marriages end in divorce and there are 2.9 million single parents (15% of all families). Blended families, with kids splitting time between their birth parents and getting to know new step-parents and step-siblings, is a new normal. Just because the adults get on, it doesn't mean their kids will, though in some cases they might actually get on better.

The chances of disagreements emerging between them and the new adult in their life, who might be as kind and nurturing as their own mum or dad but who will clearly be new and different, are high. Not forgetting that kids often like to play their parents off against each other and seem to have a sixth sense on how to go about it.

You can choose your friends but are stuck with your family. You will know them for the rest of your life, their lives. Literally.

Families have memories and sibling rivalries. They often remember all the ghastly incidents you'd prefer to forget – the time you failed your exams, got drunk and made a fool of yourself, drove the car into the hedge, broke up with 'the perfect partner'... things you've filed in the 'don't go there' bit of memory. Only start your conversation with 'I remember when...' if it's going to be positive!

Whether small families or multi-generational families with dozens of cousins, honorary uncles and aunts who are simply best mates with your parents – the only certainty is everyone in them will show up differently. Now is perhaps the time to remember that each member is likely to be living with different pressures, and their lens won't be the same as yours. We might be on different tracks but we need to be there for each other.

My message to myself is not to take my family members for granted. Continue to touch base on a regular basis, share meals and news and have real conversations. Show that I'm interested in their lives.

So how, in whatever way you define it, are the members of your own family? Are they well – healthy physically and mentally? How's their job going? School? (Few kids admit to being bullied; you need to read the signs.) When did you last speak? Are there rifts to heal?

Sometimes it's a good idea to get together outside the usual family gatherings. It makes space for a quieter, more honest catch-up!

I don't know many Von Trapp families where all the siblings merrily sing along together. Everyone arrives on the planet as a different character, developing different interests, talents and friendships along the way. We're not designed as clones. Celebrate it. In a way we need to make more effort to support those closest to us because we may primarily know them as annoying kids, sullen teens and broken-hearted lovers; or as parents who started off as gods when we were little and became less so for most of our life. We've been alongside for years and shared the challenges, triumphs, celebrations and disappointments.

A distant relative of mine had it all well planned. With the future in mind he bought three plots of land for his three children, adjacent to each other. And, no, they never ended up living their adult lives on the same street. Not even in the same continent.

There's an important lesson here. You just can't 'plan' someone else's life. Especially your children's. What is important to you is not necessarily important to them. Encourage and support their dreams, not your dreams for them. Enjoy the difference.

My father and his brother lived very different lives and rarely spoke to each other. Until, at the funeral of my uncle, my father was left to reminisce alone. I can't help thinking they were both a little sad about this, because despite their differences, if they'd made an effort to stay connected both lives would have been much happier.

The average couple meets and falls in love over a period of two years before getting married. Within the next two years they're likely to start a family if they're going to. Depending on circumstances their children leave home between 18 and 22 years later. (I know today they often bounce back but bear with me as there are always exceptions.)

So then, from the first time a couple meets to the time their children leave home is roughly 26 years. If they're then in their fifties or sixties they face the reality of spending the rest of their lives together, possibly another 25 to 30 years with increasingly declining health. It's a very common time for divorces and separations to spike.

The reality of this was brought home to me by a safari guide and anthropologist. I paraphrase from memory but the story goes pretty much like this:

"There are a lot of divorces on my safaris! As an American, most of my clients come from the US or Canada. That makes for an expensive holiday, so my clients tend to be successful and come as couples. We have game drives during the day and then camp overnight in the bush. We build a big fire to sit around and eat early, before it's too dark. Then there's the whole evening to while away and it soon becomes pretty obvious that it's the first time many couples have had a decent conversation for years. The husband has suggested the holiday; his wife has booked it. They live busy lives – the demands of work, entertaining, kids growing up. They've not really listened to each other for years and now they have long evenings to do just that. Often it doesn't end well."

The reality is they've grown apart. They no longer have much in common. They have talked but not really listened to each other, especially about their feelings. They've not invested quality time in maintaining that first mutual spark that attracted them to each other.

Your role in a partnership is not necessarily to heal family relationships as much as to keep in touch, or keep trying to look for ways and opportunities to keep communication and dialogue open. Times change, people change; they do forgive and heal.[11]

11 Common sense course for staying happily married: www.themarriage-course.org

P.S. I appreciate some people are really difficult. Perhaps narcissistic, psychopathic or even abusive. Or on a life path you feel will drag you down. You can and should forgive but you don't have to keep in touch. Prioritising your own mental and physical wellbeing comes first.

But this quote is very important:

> "It is one of the beautiful compensations of life that no man can sincerely try to help another without helping himself"
>
> Ralph Waldo Emerson

A few thoughts on forgiveness

Forgiveness is generosity. Forgiveness and moving on ought to be no-brainers. Still it is perhaps the toughest of all generous acts. Forgiving people for things they have said or done (or things you *think* they have said or done) that have made you angry, or perhaps hurt you, is hugely difficult and takes great courage. It can also be hard to forgive yourself, perhaps for not having done all that you could in a relationship. Ultimately, though, the choice is between continuing to harbour bitterness or embracing the positive impacts of healing.

It is difficult when the person you need to forgive has done something really unacceptable, or when *they* are not in a forgiving mood and you have to continue making the effort and keeping the door open. Injustices and 'alternative truths' are incredibly difficult to deal with in these situations, but there is a simple truth about forgiveness – it is an act of choice. You can choose to forgive someone for something they have done, feel the weight lifted from your shoulders and your heart, and move on. Or you can refuse forgiveness and carry the mistrust or hatred with you to your grave. A choice that means you choose to live less freely.

If you think it impossible, remember the example of South Africa's Truth and Reconciliation process or Northern Ireland's Peace and Reconciliation initiatives.

Just think for a moment about the depth of pain and the healing process – and the sheer power of reconciliation.

Forgiveness
is the
toughest
of all
generous
acts

5. Your friends

"From quiet homes and first beginning,
Out to the undiscovered ends,
There's nothing worth the wear of winning,
But laughter and the love of friends."

Hilaire Belloc

So how are your friends? Friends since childhood, best buddies you share all your secrets with. Friends made at school or uni who now live some way away. What was the bond you forged and is it still there? The few friends you know well enough to call in a crisis.

My friend Tim's 'Aam Aberdeen' story

I had booked myself onto a six-week course at the diving centre in Plymouth. My companions were a crew of die-hard diving club members and a team from the Special Boat Squadron (SBS).

At the end of the course, I was the only one staying for the last night apart from the SBS team and as darkness fell they began drinking beer followed by the opening of an expensive bottle of malt. They all stood up, poured a shot each then, noticing me, invited me to join them.

What followed has shaped my life.

"4am Aberdeen!" they shouted as they stood, raised their fists and collectively bumped them. Tentatively I joined in. Each person took a turn at toastmastering.

When we all sat down, drunk and a bit shaky, I asked my neighbour what the significance of this ritual was.

"It's like this... It's 4am and you've done something dreadful. Doesn't matter what. Who do you trust so much that you call them knowing that within five minutes they will be on their way?" He explained further, "When you look into your address book and contacts and ask yourself that question, there's very, very few you could rely on to have your back in any circumstance and, I mean *any* circumstance. You have just elected yourself to a rare gang."

I have never been called to assist that group of remarkable people, but, to this day, I get a card or a note once a year.

It got me thinking and I realised there were three such friends in my life and I took them so much for granted that I hardly stayed in contact. I was determined to improve.

Ask yourself that question and you'll realise that for all your 'fancy Dan' friends and acquaintances there are only the most precious few you can rely on totally.

From that night to this I remember my 4am Aberdeen friends and make time. You never know when you might need them or they you."

So who are the true friends you enjoy being with because you understand them and they 'get' you, share common interests, make you laugh, just click with instantly when you meet up? Those special friends you really trust?

Like for Tim, there'll likely only be a few, but among them there are bound to be some you haven't seen for ages – since they got another job, moved out of the city or to another country, got married or divorced or began a new job. (How is that job?)

Lifelong friends, the ones you have been through

a lot with, know most about and in turn know most about you and put up with you, are invaluable. And you are most likely invaluable to them. There's huge comfort in touching base with someone who knows the ups and downs you've been through and is still there for you.

Long term counts. As a friend who fought an exhausting, hugely stressful, custody battle for her children said, 'It's so nice to be with someone who knows what I've been through. I don't have to explain how I came to be where I am, because you know. There are things I will never mention to my new neighbours."

Time for a rain check. Never assume because someone's not been in touch recently they're super busy and all is well. Are they OK? Do they need a hug? If you value the friendship, get in touch.

Society gives a brave face a big tick. It took years before a long-term friend told me his brother was an addict. And for another whose life turned from being a very successful businessman to undergoing serious cancer treatment within weeks. Accidents are just that – no one plans them.

I often sum it up by saying,

"Wasting time with a friend is not wasting time."

Swapping news and just being together for no particular purpose is a true blessing and part of what friendships are all about. Coming alongside friends who are going through a difficult time is especially valuable.

Make a list of just a few to begin with. Maybe half a dozen you've not seen/caught up with for a while. Drop them a note to ask how they are, suggest a time for a proper catch-up or, if they live nearby, meet for a coffee, a walk, a meal... anything really! It's a listening role, 'listening plus' – try to avoid being the one on 'transmit'. Practise keeping quiet for a change. A friend who lives in a permanent whirlwind as a single mother of two, a small business owner also studying for a degree, someone who finds it almost impossible to take time out. Knowing someone is thinking of them – even just sending a funny GIF or meme – could make their day.

Emotions are good – they mean you are human.

We all make new friends throughout our lives, and sometimes you'll only have a short window to sense if the person you're chatting to could become significant to your life. How do you work it out? What I find invaluable is this: when you first meet someone to ask "What do you get up to when you're not being dynamic? Do you sing or are you a cold-water swimmer or..." they will laugh and reveal their interests, which you may have in common, or which may simply be unique and fascinating! I guarantee you'll have a much more enjoyable, fun conversation than when you ask, "What do you do?'

Of course not everyone's going through a difficult time, but if you don't check you'll never know. Simply say, "Hello, been thinking about you. How are things?" If the answer's "I'm fine", try "But how are you *really*?" Then wait. Trust me. You'll find it makes a difference.

The people I keep an eye on all tell me how knowing someone's thinking of them enough to touch base is a real lift when they're down, even if they choose not to open up. It's easier for them to reach out when they're feeling stronger.

OK – you don't have the time for all this? I'm willing to bet you don't remember how you know some of the folks whose phone numbers you have saved in your contacts list. Am I right? Beyond that overdue edit, here's a true story from a friend because it's fun:

> Her: "How did you become a Facebook Friend? I don't remember you."
> Him: "We had a blind date a year ago. Want to meet up again?"

Within a year of connecting again they were (and still are!) happily married!

Maybe this is the time to focus on spending more time with people you actually like, as opposed to being continually sociable for the curious purpose of being so.

Simon Sinek, an inspirational business leadership speaker and author, has a great way with words. I love his thoughts on friendship, so quote them here:

> "We live in a world where most people are ill equipped on how to be there for a friend who's struggling" – he adds that often it is not

appropriate to be a friend in 'fix-it mode'
"I'm okay, I will move forwards but allow me to mourn... I'll be fine, just hold space for me. Come and sit in the mud with me. Ask me how I'm feeling, ask me how I'm doing. Just let me vent. Just sit in the mud with me..."[12]

I love 'Just sit in the mud with me". I've 'sat in the mud' with many people, some with cancer diagnoses that at first they certainly didn't want anyone to know about, others who have faced very emotional relationship issues, financial problems or changes in their work and career. Sometimes I have been able to link them to another person who can help – but mostly I have just kept in touch regularly. A phone call, a message, a coffee, a walk. We have all been there and I am sure that you recognise that place too. When people are feeling vulnerable they often don't want to talk about their problems, but if you don't press them directly they will gently open up in their own time.

12 Simon Sinek on 'sitting in the mud': https://youtu.be/7md9c8MxIOs

Finally, a tip on "I'm fine"...

This is almost certainly the response when you ask people if you can help them in any way.

Does this ring a bell? Is this you? Are you completely useless at putting your hand up and asking for help, even when you really need it?

I've done it myself! I've even written a book or two about generosity. And often when someone has asked me "Can I help you?", I've replied, "No, honestly, thank you, it's ok, I am *fine*."

One day someone who knew me well told me, with mild frustration, to stop it. That there was no point banging on about being 'generous' when I wouldn't accept generosity from others. They wanted to help me, and I wouldn't allow them to.

If you have a problem, or need help sometimes – and who doesn't? – put your hand up and share it with a friend.

As the old saying goes, 'a problem shared is a problem halved'.

You know how good it feels to give. Let others feel that too by accepting help when it is offered. In effect, be generous with allowing others to feel the goodness of being generous themselves.

6.

Your work

> "It's amazing what you can accomplish if you do not care who takes the credit."
>
> Harry S Truman

In his book *The Age of Unreason*, published in 1989, Charles Handy, a highly respected management guru, first introduced the idea of a portfolio career. He forecast that there would no longer be such a thing as a secure job. The world was, and indeed is, changing so quickly that the idea of a lifetime career is well and truly buried. The average life of a business is only sixteen years, and structures change so often that even when employed you may well have to reapply for your job while you're there. And getting jobs when you're over fifty will become increasingly hard.

The world Handy predicted is already here but I doubt in the way he imagined. Millions of people have so-called 'precarious jobs', zero-hours contracts and/

or are juggling multiple jobs;[13] around 1 in 20 do freelance work full time for a living and you can multiply that by three when you add in part-time working:[14] makers on Etsy, sellers on eBay and Vinted; and once you get to 10,000 followers you can earn about £100 for a podcast. For every influencer or podcaster earning a decent living, most need a traditional job as well.[15]

13 Precarious work stats: www.ucl.ac.uk/news/2024/nov/almost-one-ten-uk-workers-increasingly-trapped-precarious-work

14 Freelancing stats: archimedia accounts.co.uk/freelancing-statistics-uk

15 Influencer earnings: www.limelight digital.co.uk/how-much-do-influencers-make

Handy, on the other hand, purposefully developed what he called a portfolio life, a collection of different jobs, some paid, some unpaid but useful. He and his wife Elizabeth divided each year into three parts. One third they worked to earn the income their family needed for their normal expenditure – food, mortgage payments, school fees, holidays etc. One third they did something that really interested them – he wrote various best-selling books (which he actually discovered was very hard work!) – and the final third they dedicated to pro bono work – helping good causes for nothing. They called this 'maximising their lives, not their income'.

As I explained in the introduction of this book, after sleeping for a third of your life on earth, your work (the official kind) takes up the next highest proportion at 13% ("No, it's more!" I hear you cry). That means nearly half your life is spent asleep or at work.

It's not down to me to judge whether your work is useful and productive – being locked down for the Covid-19 pandemic was a wake-up call for how much we depend on essential, often 'invisible' workers. So thank you to the millions of teachers, medical professionals, carers, street cleaners, bus drivers, firefighters and more.

Work provides essential income, keeps life going and at its best gives purpose and dignity. Even if, it seems, great and supportive working environments seem to be all too few. Research company Gallup conducted a global poll in 2022. It found that of a billion people in full-time work worldwide, only 15% are emotionally engaged with their work, leaving a staggering 85% unhappy.[16] A LinkedIn poll which found that 85% of respondents don't like their job validated the Gallup findings.

16 Gallup poll results on work satisfaction: www.gallup.com/learning/event/4907504/EventDetails.aspx

Given it's what we spend most of our life doing after sleeping, what a sad state of affairs. We need supportive colleagues who understand the pressures we're under. And to be supportive back.

Diversity of every sort is known to enrich the workplace, so allow for it. As scientists learn more, neurological differences in particular are being seen as normal variations in the way our brains are wired – so the different ways of thinking, learning, processing information and interacting with the world that impact about one in seven of us (think ADHD, dyslexia, autism and more) bring unique perspectives that enormously enrich our world and work. Think Leonardo da Vinci and Albert Einstein. While no one can be totally sure, it's thought they both displayed characteristics of ADHD. Richard Branson doesn't see his dyslexia and ADHD as a disability. Greta Thunberg has described her Asperger's as her superpower.

So... how is life at work? How are your colleagues/fellow workers? Do you know? Do you *really* know them at all beyond what they do? The personal pressures they are under? Believe me, these will have a very real impact on their daily lives and work.

Here's an anecdote from a large, highly successful advertising agency. The new receptionist suggested an informal weekly 'cakes and tea' break for people to mingle and chat. 'Cakes and tea' happened for several months. Unlikely connections were forged as people enjoyed getting to know each other as people, not just their jobs. Until more senior management debunked the idea as a total waste of precious work time. It stopped. And in the following months productivity and morale across the board were measurably down.

People show up at work, but it's never their whole life. It's not rocket science to know non-work stuff has a huge impact. The imminent arrival of a baby or the end of a relationship; debt, moving home, illness, family ups and downs. Very few people can block everything out and most bottle it up, which isn't great for them or the working environment.

Of course, the reverse is also true. When you spend too much time being 'incredibly busy at work' you can miss sports days, school plays, anniversaries, weddings, birthday celebrations and a friend's milestone event. You can't rewind the clock or remake the memories. You were just not there.

“No one on their deathbed ever said, ‘I wish I’d spent more time at work”

Often attributed to 92-year-old Massachusetts native Arnold Zack

Are you one of the 85% or the 15%? Assuming you have the privilege of mobility and choice in what you do, is work fun, fulfilling and challenging in equal measure? Are you valued? Paid fairly? Or does your boss and the management at best not communicate the vision or your role in it, or are they, at their worst, toxic? Would you rather be anywhere else or are you still looking for work after endless failed job applications?

If you're loving work, your memo to yourself is to make space to check that those you work with feel supported and love it too.

If you're a boss the question is, "What do you need from me to help you do this job really well?" (this is one of the central messages from Robert Greenleaf's work on 'servant leadership'). People who really listen build great teams. A very successful CEO whose staff couldn't speak highly enough of him shared this advice: "Always employ the best people. Be very clear about the result you want them to achieve and then let them get on with it. Don't interfere."

In addition to this he was simply wonderful with people. I asked him *why* he was so loved and respected – what about having to 'let people go' or tell them their work 'wasn't good enough'? His answer has stayed with me all my life:

"It's the manner not the matter."

People always know themselves when their work isn't going well (the matter). It's the way you talk to them and treat them, especially when they leave, that is important (the manner). That is why he was admired throughout the company and indeed the business world he was in.

Wisdom from another age:

"Go to the people
Live with them
Learn from them
Love them
Start with what they know
Build on what they have
But of the best leaders
When their job is done
The task accomplished
The people will say
'We have done it ourselves.'"

Lao Tzu, sixth-century Chinese philosopher

Life's short, so this is to encourage you not to put up with something that takes up so much time and makes you unhappy. One way of clarifying all this is a quick personal audit...

Personal audit

Make four lists – and do include personal things such as singing, swimming and reading:

1. What am I really/exceptionally good at?
    -
    -
    -
2. What am I really bad at/not very good at?
    -
    -
    -
3. What do I really enjoy doing?
    -
    -
    -
4. What do I not like doing?
    -
    -
    -

Then put a line through your answers to 2 and 4 – what you are not good at and don't enjoy doing – and make every effort to avoid or delegate them forever. A tip – if you don't want to do something someone really wants you to do, do it really badly once!

Now focus on what you love doing and are good at. Does the thought bring you joy? Or might it?

Perfection and Procrastination lead to Paralysis – and are the silent killers of many dreams

Changing to a new world that you may thrive in isn't always easy. It takes courage, determination and time. Every career/role includes difficult or boring bits and times – and nothing worthwhile can be achieved without overcoming challenges. It takes energy and commitment to sort out the complicated issues in the 'too difficult to deal with' drawer.

When you have settled on a couple of areas/ideas you think you would like to explore, get in touch with people who work in those worlds for an informal chat: "I am thinking of moving to work in..." – it doesn't matter where. What matters are the sensible insights and advice you'll receive, the opportunities not yet advertised, other useful people introduced. You'll begin to understand the lay of the land and every connection will build a clearer picture. You owe it to yourself to find work you love, with colleagues who care and are supportive. Remember, after sleeping, it'll take up most of your life.

Be brave and impress everyone you meet with your determination and curiosity to find out more. In my experience it's often fear that holds people back, so just go for it.

You will probably become excited again!

And if you're one of the many who's working somewhere you really don't want to be out of necessity to pay the bills, it's still possible to try and rebalance your life, to focus on spending more time with your family and friendships, on your hobbies and other interests that will bring you joy elsewhere.

7.

People you don't (or hardly) know

'Be not inhospitable to strangers, lest they be angels in disguise' –

A sign in Shakespeare & Company, the wonderful bookshop in Paris that provides a bed and supper for aspiring writers in return for their help in the shop.

There are several much-viewed YouTube clips, filmed in different countries, where the same man trips and falls badly on a busy city pavement. Twice. The first time he's dressed as an office worker and several passers-by stop to help him. The same guy then repeats his fall dressed as someone who could be homeless. You've already guessed what happened. People walked round and avoided him.

Closer to home you probably know a few people who it's easy to politely ignore because they're difficult, not good company and best to avoid. If everyone thinks like you do, they are likely to be living a very hard and quite friendless, lonely life. Brightening up their day is easier than you think. Put simply, you can empathise and just be kind. A word of encouragement or doing something small could mean more than you will ever know.

We like to label people and rest secure in the world of 'us not them'. People with disabilities, refugees, elderly people, those with mental health issues, kids, people with a non-traditional hairstyle even. Making fun of someone might boost your self-esteem, but when you break the mould and engage, you'll likely be surprised. You are not actually going to have a series of 'aha' moments – it takes time to understand a person's life until you hear their story. But you will learn a little more.

The Biblical parable of the Good Samaritan is well known. Jesus tells a lawyer that he should love his neighbour as much as he loves himself. "Who is my neighbour?" replies the man (they can be quite pedantic, these lawyers).

The parable is worth reading:

> "A man was travelling from Jerusalem to Jericho when he was attacked by robbers, who stripped and beat him, leaving him half dead. The next person to arrive was a priest who saw the half-dead man and passed by on the other side of the road. Then came a Levite. He did exactly the same. The third passer-by was a Samaritan. When he saw the man, he was moved with compassion, came to him

> and treated and bound up his wounds. Then he put him on his own animal and brought him to an inn so that he could take care of him properly. When the Samaritan had to leave the next day, he gave the innkeeper two days' money to look after the injured man's needs with instructions to carry on doing whatever was necessary, and assurances that if more money was needed, the Samaritan would pay the extra on his return journey."

Having told the story, Jesus asked the lawyer which of the three had been a good neighbour to the injured man.

> "He who showed mercy."
> "Then go and do likewise."

The lesson from the Good Samaritan is totally relevant to the world we live in today, regardless of whether you're a person of faith or not. One of the key points is the contrast. The priest and the Levite were highly regarded religious leaders (Levites helped priests in the temple). Touching the half-dead man risked making them unclean so they didn't hesitate to put their self-interests first and left him to die. The Samaritan wasn't highly regarded at all. He was one of society's outcasts and a stranger in the neighbourhood, yet he was the one who broke his journey, stopped and helped. The despised, lowest-of-the-low Samaritan went above and beyond. He bound the wounds, carried the half-dead man to a place of safety, paid the innkeeper to lodge him and promised to return and pay more if needed.

It was an extraordinary act of kindness. Those who should and could have helped didn't. The unmentioned question the priest and the Levite asked themselves was: "If I stop to help this man, what will happen to me?"

The Samaritan, however, asked: "If I don't stop to help this man what will happen to him?"

Now own up. How many times have you deliberately passed by on the other side?

How often have you ignored someone's request for help, or realised someone was having a difficult time – at work, at home or health-wise – and avoided asking them about it for fear of getting too close?

Have you avoided someone because you see 'homeless', 'alcoholic', 'mentally ill', 'mad', 'a waster' – and simply written them off? You perhaps hurried on with your own life, feeling you didn't have the bandwidth to be kind. You had enough problems of your own, you felt uncomfortable or were just very busy. And anyway... surely someone else will step in.

I repeat: at different times in our lives we are all insecure and anxious, dealing with our own problems and challenges. All we are asked to do is to spare a thought, and as importantly a little of our time, to come alongside others, speak to them, show interest and care. To be a better human.

“Three things in human life are important: the first is to be kind; the second is to be kind; and the third is to be kind.”

Henry James

Make a mental note: "The next time I see a Big Issue seller I will actually talk to them for a few minutes and ask them about their life, rather than 'graciously' buy a copy of the magazine and hurry on."

Incidentally, your everyday interaction with *all* shop and bar staff, waiters, delivery people, receptionists and everyone else in the service industry will brighten up their day and yours immeasurably. 'Thank you's, 'how are you today's, 'thank you for being here's – they all make the world go round a little bit easier.

The story of the starfish

A man was walking along a beach. The sun was shining and it was a beautiful day. In the distance he could see a young girl going back and forth between the surf's edge and the dry sand. Then he noticed hundreds of starfish stranded. The girl was hurling them one by one back into the sea.

The man was struck by the apparent futility of the task. There were far too many starfish to save. But, as he approached, the girl continued picking up starfish one by one and throwing them into the surf.

"You must be crazy," said the man when he reached her. "There are thousands of miles of beach covered with starfish. You can't possibly make a difference."

The girl held the man's gaze. She then stooped down, picked up one more starfish and threw it back into the ocean. She turned back to the man and smiled. "It made a difference to that one!"

8.

Our world

"I always say that however good or bad the system is, people will fall through the cracks. I want to be among the people who catch them."

A note sent to Jaime Thurston – founder of 52 Lives

A very good friend suggested that I meet Jaime, the founder of 52 Lives, a registered charity in the UK that aims to help people while asking for nothing in return. So I obliged and found myself totally inspired by her and her work.[17]

17 52 Lives: www.52-lives.org

Jaime's story

"In 2013, I came across a wanted ad on a website. It was a lady looking for a rug to cover her broken floor, as her children were cutting their feet. I learnt more about her and discovered she had escaped a horrible domestic situation. She and her children had been homeless and she was in a very dark place. I thought, if people knew about her, I know so many who would be willing to help. So I emailed my friends and family, collected various bits and pieces and delivered it all to her one day. She was in tears at the door – not because of the things I was giving her, but because she couldn't believe that complete strangers would be willing to help her. She later sent me an email saying 'you have restored my faith in humanity'.

That's when the idea for 52 Lives was born. I wanted to do more – so I set up a Facebook page called 52 Lives, with the aim of helping to change one person's life every week of the year.

Eleven years on, and we have almost 100,000 supporters across our social media channels and we have an incredible, loyal community of kind people who come together every week to spread kindness to those who need it. We provide practical support, but all the people we help say the same thing – that it's not just the things we give them that change their life, it's the kindness – the fact that people who are total strangers care about them. We let people know they're not alone.

A lady called Jo sends cards every week for the people we help. This week, I saw one of Jo's cards was addressed to me. I wanted to share some of what she wrote, as it sums up so perfectly what we do and explains why she loves being part of this community. She said, "I always say that however good or bad the system is, people will fall through the cracks. I want to be among the people who catch them."

Fewer people are watching the news. Including me. Not well-investigated journalism, but fake news when you can discern it, views on X or Telegram or other social media. It's increasingly difficult to easily identify real news these days. To state the obvious, the problems of the world are vast, serious and seemingly insurmountable and while the latest crisis may dominate, it doesn't mean the others have gone away.

All this may well make you feel, with some justification, depressed, helpless and hopeless. So I'd like to remind you that you have enormous power to be both helpful and hopeful. When you nurture your caring side you'll sleep better at night. This is a call to use your free time to get stuck in to help something (or someone) you really care about.

Some years ago I interviewed a long-standing friend about his own generosity and philanthropy – Dr Frederick Mulder CBE. Fred's own success has enabled him to help more charities and people than anyone else I know personally and, importantly, he's found a great way to enjoy the process and has encouraged thousands of others to enjoy it too. I asked him what inspired him. He said:

> "Everyone wants to make a positive difference in the world... If you are fortunate enough to have the financial wherewithal, it is a wonderful thing to be able to do. Making someone happy, comfortable, feel loved or accepted or safe is a very powerful thing. There are certain things that you want to see done in giving terms that are about your own values and the values you would like to see embedded in the world. You can't do it because you don't have the skills, are too busy doing something else or don't have the time. Then you find wonderful people who *are* doing it and you think, 'Oh my god, that needs to be done, but I can't do it; I'll help those people to do it' – that's a much better way."

Alongside his personal philanthropy, Fred is a founder of The Funding Network, one of the earliest adopters of crowdfunding.[18] Wonderfully upbeat social evenings are organised for small social enterprises and charities to pitch to an interested and interesting audience. Think of *Dragon's Den* and then imagine a positive, encouraging forum where the guests donate small sums of money and together crowdfund thousands of pounds in under an hour. Every charity chosen to pitch is a winner. Local ones, high-impact

18 The Funding Network: www.thefundingnetwork.org.uk

strategic ones, ones with stories that are so moving it's a privilege to be in the same room and meet the speakers. An even better feeling when you just can't help but put your hand up to offer £50, £100 or more for one or two of the causes. Each one raises between £6,000 to £10,000 during the evening and often more.

To paraphrase Fred, "We eat together, dance together, play together, but all too often when we give, we give alone."

Over the last 20 years The Funding Network has raised over £17 million for 2,435 small charities in the UK and Ireland. It now operates in 27 countries, and the international organisation has raised an additional £7.2 million through 374 events.

All because Fred and three friends had an idea to make giving a fun activity which they could enjoy together.

Isn't it time to engage enthusiastically and proactively with others in saving the world or at least your part of it? The small part of it that is within reach is fine. Putting your hand up builds that important, intangible and elusive component of our lives that is about community and connection.

Larger well-established charities do very important work. Still, you might prefer to support and become involved in a smaller organisation that's growing, or something local. It'll vary depending on your other commitments and of course, whether you can offer skills or time, and the level of money or time you are comfortable giving.

Either way – here's a word from someone who has built a successful charity and spent many, many years helping others (yes 'tis me!):

If you are one of those who still twitter on about how you "want every penny of the money I donate to a charity to go to the cause, not the overheads'... you really need to get a grip and have a serious word with yourself.

And then watch Dan Pallotta's strikingly intelligent TED talk, 'The way we think about charity is dead wrong', in which he argues persuasively that charities must use some of their income to fundraise for more funds and to grow their management structure to be able make a larger impact on the social issue they are tackling. He says:

> "In the for-profit sector, the more value you produce, the more money you can make. But we don't like nonprofits to use money to incentivise people to produce more in social service. We have a visceral reaction to the idea that anyone would make very much money helping other people. Interestingly, we don't have a visceral reaction to the notion that people would make a lot of money not helping other people.
>
> "You know, you want to make 50 million dollars selling violent video games to kids, go for it. We'll put you on the cover of *Wired* magazine. But you want to make half a million dollars trying to cure kids of malaria, and you're considered a parasite yourself."[19]

19 Dan Pallotta's TED Talk on the way we think about charity: www.ted.com/talks/dan_pallotta_the_way_we_think_about_charity_is_dead_wrong

He goes on:

> "Our generation does not want its epitaph to read, 'We kept charity overhead low.' We want it to read that we changed the world, and that part of the way we did that was by changing the way we think about these things."

So the next time you're looking at a charity, don't ask about the rate of their overheads. Ask about the scale of their dreams – their Apple/Google/Amazon-scale dreams, how they measure their progress toward those dreams and what resources they need to make them come true, regardless of what the overheads are. Does the overhead percentage matter if these problems are actually getting solved?

People will always fall through the cracks. Who could you catch?

Here are two more examples of individuals who've started small and then kept going – transforming lives and their communities.

Lavinia: Grandfriends

Lavinia loved being around her grandparents when she was growing up and wished that for her children too. The idea blossomed into a local charity: Grandfriends – The Company of Elders.[20] Grandfriends connects trained elders (a loose definition – you choose) with primary school children to chat and do fun activities that take the kids off their smartphones, something both teachers and parents are really happy about! From another perspective the positive intergenerational connections help reduce loneliness and isolation, building the sort of strong, mutually supportive community we all wish for. A simple idea which could take root anywhere.

20 Grandfriends: www.grandfriends.uk

Pam Warhurst: Incredible Edibles

"If you eat, you're in," says Pam. She and a couple of friends started a community initiative, Incredible Edibles, back in 2008.[21] The question they asked upfront was, 'What can we do that will unify this town, Todmorden in West Yorkshire, involve everyone and encourage people to help themselves?' The

21 Incredible Edibles: www.incredibleedible.org.uk

answer was food. With no budget and 'no flipping strategy document', the community has gradually turned their small, quite run-down market town into a place where herbs, fruit and veg are planted in every patch of spare earth available. The mantra 'If you eat, you're in', as well as the idea of the three spinning plates (education, business, food) to regenerate a town, has spread around the world. Pam's two key messages are particularly worth highlighting: the first is the power of small actions, and the second is that empowering people to do their own thing shifts the dial. Put simply, it works. And has now spread to communities across the world, from New Zealand to Japan, India to Brazil and even the USA. From a kitchen table. With no budget, no bureaucracy and 'no flipping strategy document'!

I could name more, but both of these examples show how, when people connect and look after each other, even at very simple levels, they can change their part of the world to become a better place.

If we are to be really human, living life to the full, it's not difficult – it is just a case of taking action at any level that seems possible, with generosity and care. As one of the nearly 70 million people who live in the UK, I don't want to leave it all to local-level, cash-strapped, regional or national government while I have the ability to make the country I live in a little bit better myself. With friends it would be even more fun and invaluable.

As I am writing this, Trussell, an anti-poverty charity and community of food banks, published research reporting that more than nine million people in the UK experience levels of poverty and hunger so extreme they are vulnerable to reliance on charity food handouts.[22]

22 Food bank stats: www.theguardian.com/society/2024/oct/09/britons-vulnerable-reliance-food-banks-research-finds; The Trussell Trust: www.trussell.org

Isn't that unbelievable and scandalous in a wealthy and so-called civilised country?

“What we think
or what we
know or what
we believe is in
the end of little
consequence.
The only thing
of consequence
is what we do”

John Ruskin

9.
The power of kindness

> 'Do unto others as you would have them do unto you'
>
> Gospel of Matthew, 7:12.

Treating other people as you would like to be treated and helping those less fortunate than yourself isn't my idea. It's wisdom that's been handed down for literally thousands of years. Something that can be found in every culture, society and faith. The earliest reference I could find to it was in 1800 BC. It's funny, even sad, that we give it so little attention. Put simply, doesn't it make huge sense to be kind to each other? To encourage and build each other up?

Throughout history and prehistory, the great philosophers and religious leaders have all had two key teachings in common.

1. The Golden Rule: their own version of what is written in Matthew's gospel. What is now known as the Golden Rule was first found in Egyptian society around 1800 BC.
2. We all have a responsibility to help others, especially those less fortunate than ourselves. This is embedded across all major global beliefs and indigenous societies and practised among almost every known culture worldwide.

Interestingly, while it may seem that we live in an increasingly individualist and faithless world, the facts may surprise you.[23] Of the just over eight billion people in the world, around 75% belong to one of the major world faiths, before including the many smaller religions and indigenous cultures. Of the eight billion (at the latest count), 2.4 billion are Christian, 1.9 billion Muslim, 1.6 billion Hindu and 500 million Buddhist. Some research suggests secular non-believers and atheists total 1.1 billion. If my maths is right that's 14% – so 86% of the global population believe in something bigger than themselves.

23 British beliefs: yougov.co.uk/topics/society/trackers/brits-beliefs-about-gods

And all major faiths share those two extremely important core teachings, of which the Golden Rule is the first.

The history of the Golden Rule

(As researched & published by Kim Polman and Stephen Vasconcellos-Sharpe)[24]

24 *Imaginal Cells: Visions of Transformation* edited by Kim Polman and Stephen Vasconcellos-Sharpe, 2017

- In **ancient Egypt** (c. 1800 BC) the Story of the Eloquent Peasant says: "Do to the doer to cause that he do."
- The Chinese philosopher **Confucius** (551–479 BC) puts it nicely: "Don't do to others what you don't want them to do to you."
- **Taoism**, also from China (c. 500 BC): "Regard your neighbour's gain as your gain and your neighbour's loss as your loss."
- **Hinduism:** *Mahabharata* book 13, *Anushasana Parva* (400 BC): "In happiness and misery, in the agreeable and the disagreeable, one should judge the effects as if they came to one's own self."
- **Judaism:** from the Babylonian *Talmud*, Shabbat 31a, attributed to the Elder Hillel (c. 100 BC): "That which is hateful to you, do not do to your fellow; that is the whole Torah; the rest is interpretation."
- **Christianity:** Matthew 7:12 (c. 85 AD): "Treat others as you want to be treated, for this sums up the Law of the prophets."
- **Islam:** Prophet Mohammed via several Hadiths (610 AD): "None of us is a true believer unless he wishes for his brother what he wishes for himself."

Helping less fortunate members of society

It seems superfluous to mention that even with thousands of years of wisdom, the consistent message of the Golden Rule is too often ignored. So, let's turn to the second important teaching – again universally shared. It is the importance of, and responsibility to, help the less fortunate members of society.

Islam teaches that everything belongs to Allah, with wealth being held by human beings in trust. One of the key pillars of Islam, *Zakat*, meaning both 'purification' and 'growth', is taught in the Quran as obligatory. It's the amount of money that every mentally stable, free and financially able Muslim must pay to support others in need. Setting aside a proportion of what you have purifies you. Cutting back on your needs balances and encourages new growth. For most Muslims this involves an annual payment of 2.5% of capital over a certain threshold to others in need.

Hindu culture teaches that God could visit your home at any time, and when he does, he'll come as a stranger to whom you must offer food and shelter. If you really want to know God, he is in the strangers. No one should leave your house without at least a glass of water.

> "Teach this triple truth to all: a generous heart, kind speech and a life of service and compassion are the things which renew humanity."
>
> Gautama Buddha

The **Buddhist** concept of joy arises when someone regards all human beings with loving kindness and rejoices in their good fortune. By overcoming resentment, envy and jealousy, and finding inspiration in the happiness and accomplishment of others, an individual can begin to understand how solid and genuine shared happiness is. Buddha saw *dana* – generosity of spirit, giving and receiving from the heart – as both the generous act of giving and the gift itself. In Buddhism, generosity and kindness are skills and practices to be cultivated and nurtured for us all to thrive.

Everyone acknowledges that we are more than a bundle of flesh and bones. There is something in each of us that speaks to a spiritual element we don't quite understand. So this is about paying more attention to what our hearts are telling us and what millennia of teachings have told us too.

The **Christian** teaching of Jesus calls for reckless generosity. In the story of the widow's mite (Luke 21:1–4), he singles out not the rich putting large amounts into the temple offering, but a widow who gave a tiny amount:

> "I tell you the truth, this poor widow has put more into the treasury than all the others. They gave out of their wealth; but she out of her poverty, put in everything – all she had to live on."

For those who don't follow the teachings of organised religions, there are mindfulness, meditation and a whole host of practices that slow you down, clear your mind and enable you to connect with that inner part of yourself that science hasn't yet managed to explain, and they are gaining traction. A 2025 YouGov poll suggests over half of us (56% to be precise) believe in God, gods or some higher spiritual power while about a third (35%) don't.

Regardless of whether you are a person of faith or none, it seems fairly clear that if we all followed the Golden Rule, treating others as we would wish to be treated and sharing what we have, we would all live happier and more purposeful lives.

John Sweeney's generosity journey

"27 March 2013. I'm lying awake at 3.30 am, reading about this old tradition from Naples called Café Cepesos. Somebody buys a cup of coffee as a gesture of goodwill for someone else. Perhaps the person behind you in the queue, or just pay for two and leave the choice of who gets a free coffee to the barista. I'd never drunk a cup of coffee in my life, so I did what any normal 28-year-old failed plumber would do and started reaching out to Facebook pages, tweeting about it to media people and it caught fire. Stories were coming in and lots of people were talking about the importance of being kind in a simple way.

This was changing people. Like it was giving people permission to be kind and generous. It was becoming infectious.

Quickly about 60,000 people and about 100 cafes signed up to 'Suspended Coffees' on a dedicated Facebook page. We made international media, with *Huffington Post*, the *Times* and the *Guardian* all writing about it.

And I found myself the spokesperson. Saying that kindness could change the world.

When the Covid pandemic began we had over half a million followers on social media. Over 4,000 cafés in 34 different countries actively doing it. Like we regularly reached 50 million people a month. Our surveys estimated over 10 million Suspended Coffees had been given out across the world. Ridiculously huge numbers.

Then Covid came and it took a hit. Until, out of the blue I got this weird email: 'I'm with the TED team. We're writing a book about generosity and we'd love to feature your story.'

We chatted and then, for a chunk of time, nothing. Till another random email from TED founder Chris Anderson. 'We've included your story, we're hosting this event to launch the book and we'd love you to join, to be one of the heroes we highlight on the night.'

We met, did a podcast and I gave away a

bunch of Chris's books to strangers on the streets of London and filmed their reactions. Which seemed to impress Chris. My hustle was making Londoners want to stop and tell stories about kindness and generosity.

Chris then basically said, 'Look, I want you to work on a project that can possibly change the world. It's centred round kindness. Can you help me make this a reality?'

That's how I came to be working on Drop Dead Generous,[25] a social experiment to encourage people to pay it forward. Anyone can apply for $500 if they've a great idea to pay it forward. I'm sending to people all over – Uganda, Texas, Brazil, China, connecting with people one to one, encouraging them to think about kindness and generosity differently. To be creative, imaginative and do something they would never normally do. A social experiment based on trust. The money's yours. Make an impact, change people's lives. Tell us your stories to inspire more people.

Hopefully it's something that will catch fire and spread throughout the world. And maybe, when the money runs out, others will top it up."

25 Drop Dead Generous: www.dropdeadgenerous.org/about-us

10.

Success – and your significance

> "Most men lead lives of quiet desperation and go to their graves with their song still inside them."
>
> Inspired by Henry David Thoreau

> "Being successful doesn't necessarily make you great. What makes you great is when you reach back and help somebody else become great."
>
> Joel Osteen

Success is great. To be able to use your talents to the full to become successful in your chosen way. If you make considerable amounts of money and become financially 'wealthy' perhaps it was after years of hard work. Including moments when you thought you would fail, prioritised a deadline or solving the latest work crisis over family and friend occasions like your children's sports days, a best friend's birthday and social events. For some it will have cost you key personal relationships and even your marriage. For others it will be at great cost to your health.

While society applauds these people and celebrates their success, it's important we should also ask what they do for others. Ask them, "What amount of money is 'enough'?"

It's easy to be always busy and completely caught up with your professional or financial ambitions and that uneasy feeling that whoever's in the next desk is doing better, earning more, so you need to keep up and get promoted to earn more as well. And then more. And more. And more. It's possible to miss the point of life altogether and fail to be remotely useful to anyone: the slippery path to being an absent parent, partner or friend. And if, being well-intentioned and of fundamentally good heart, you manage to help people it's often as an afterthought – a hastily made donation when someone asks.

Alain de Botton once gently mocked visible success:

> "Next time you see someone driving a Ferrari don't think 'this is someone who is incredibly greedy', think of them as someone who is incredibly vulnerable and in need of love. Feel sympathy rather than contempt."

'Noblesse oblige' is a formal 19th-century French phrase that refers to the idea that someone with power and influence should use their social position to help other people.

Charles Dickens recognised all this when he wrote *A Christmas Carol*. Remember Scrooge?

> "Oh! But he was a tight-fisted hand at the grindstone, Scrooge! A squeezing, wrenching, grasping, scraping, clutching, covetous old sinner. Hard and sharp as a flint, from which no steel had ever struck out generous fire: secret, self-contained and solitary as an oyster. The cold within him froze his old features, nipped his pointed nose, shrivelled his cheek, stiffened his gait... he carried his own low temperature always about with him."

It takes three ghostly visits for Scrooge to see the error of his ways. Finally, through the ghost of Christmas Yet to Come, he hears colleagues discussing his own funeral: "'It's likely to be a cheap funeral' – says one – 'for upon my life I don't know of anybody who will go to it'."

Scrooge, not so keen on that as a legacy, sees the light and resolves to lead a more generous life. And in writing about him Dickens reflects a universal truth: the unhappy may mock, but that should not deflect those who are doing something to improve the world.

> "He became as good a friend, as good a master and as good a man as the good old

> city knew, or any other good old city, town or borough in the good old world. Some people laughed to see the alteration in him, but he let them laugh, and little heeded them... His own heart laughed and that was quite enough for him."

In conversations with the many people I have met who've 'made it' and are wondering what to do next, my approach usually goes something like this. "You've done incredibly well, but perhaps the reason we're chatting is because you should be asking yourself the important question 'Has what I've done been significant?' Do you feel you now have 'enough'?"

There is a huge gap between success and significance. Significance is about living a useful life, recognising how fortunate you are, using your resources to help others and being worthwhile. We can all think immediately of people we know who have either had, or who continue to have, a positive influence not only on our lives but on many others around them, with a ripple effect going further. They are the significant ones, the people who leave their thumbprint on the world.

It's not all about money. Where would we be without volunteers using their time, talents and skills? School governors, hospital visitors, people clearing local parks, fundraising for great causes, helping out at food banks and homeless shelters. Tot it up and 27% of everyone over 15 volunteers every year. And that's before we begin to think about people who just lend an informal helping hand – shopping, offering a lift, helping with childcare... add that in and almost half of us (46%) are helping out.[26]

26 Volunteers in numbers: www.ncvo.org.uk/news-and-insights/news-index/uk-civil-society-almanac-2024/volunteering

Research in many countries over the years has proved what we already know in our hearts – that helping others makes us more content and happier people ourselves. In truth we probably didn't need the research to know that people with a passion for work that has a positive impact on others – nursing, teaching, music, theatre, writing and more – never expect to earn a fortune, but mostly love the life they've chosen.

If you ask people to recall an act of kindness that they have received recently, they can always remember something. Often it is the small acts that both surprise and touch them. It is also one of life's rather wonderful blessings that often the less other people know of your kindness, the better you feel. A small act, shared between just two people, can be truly special. And so simple to do.

As you are reading this, pause for a moment and think about an act of kindness you received. How did you feel and why did it matter to you?

A known face, a kind word: Terry's story

Terry is a gardener; for many years he played for his village football team and is a member of the local pub bowling league. He lives in the same village he was born in, which – by some wonderful stroke of fate – is also the village to which this author's parents finally moved.

He's a very normal bloke, except for his exceptional generosity, which he dismisses with an embarrassed smile. One of his jobs was to help my elderly parents with their garden, mowing the lawn and keeping the hedges down when it became too much for them. For the last ten years of my mother's life, when she was in her eighties and nineties and living alone, he was also her rock.

Officially, Terry came once a week for a couple of hours. Unofficially, he popped in twice a day. Every day. Just passing by for a cup of tea at around five and back again at around eight for "the final round-up". Doors locked, cats fed, curtains closed, mother safe and OK.

In winter, the hot-water bottle would be filled and the bed warmed (for 'health and safety' reasons, this was outside the remit of the visiting carers). At one stage, the hard-pressed local authority suggested they cut back on the evening carers' visits because "your gardener comes, doesn't he?" "Yes, but it's not his job or his responsibility. He does it out of the kindness of his heart," my mother would respond. And we didn't pay him, because time and again he refused the offer.

When my mother's daily routine reduced to moving between her bedroom and the armchair, Terry was the constant presence in her life. Much more constant than I was able to be, living a hundred-plus miles away. A known face, a kind word. Every day, twice a day, as regular as clockwork.

My phone would ring: "Terry's late, do you think he's alright?" or "I'm worried about Terry, he hasn't come yet." I can count on the fingers of one hand the days he didn't come round without letting my mother know in advance – and there was always a reason, such as there had been a wedding or a funeral which had lasted longer than expected.

In 2023 Henstridge Parish Council thanked Terry for his wonderful work: "We all know Terry Pulling – a very familiar figure around Henstridge either on his bike or wheeling his lawn mower around the village. But how many of us realised that August this year was the 40th anniversary of Terry working for Henstridge Parish Council. 40 years of keeping this village looking neat and tidy! Born & bred in Henstridge he is a village institution – dedicated, reliable, conscientious and hard-working. Congratulations and many thanks from all of us Terry, we hope you carry on for many years to come."

Thank you, Terry. I am forever indebted to you, though you will brush away the compliment. You are a truly generous gentleman in every way.

Honestly, no one at your funeral or memorial service will ever remember, much less discuss, how many houses, cars, designer clothes you owned, never mind your private plane or wonderful yacht. They will all talk about and remember your acts of kindness and the positive impact you had on each one of their lives.

“What you do for yourself dies with you. What you do for others’ lives on forever.”

Sir Ken Robinson

Melinda Gates, co-founder of the Bill and Melinda Gates Foundation, when interviewed in 2025 was asked, "Are we all doomed?" She answered:

> "Optimism isn't a passive expectation that things will get better on their own – it's a belief that we can make them better. So no, I don't think so at all. There are too many people working too hard to tear down barriers and keep progress moving forward. The best part of my job is having a front row seat to all that work."

It Couldn't Be Done

Somebody said that it couldn't be done
But he with a chuckle replied
That "maybe it couldn't," but he would be one
Who wouldn't say so till he'd tried.
So he buckled right in with the trace of a grin
On his face. If he worried he hid it.
He started to sing as he tackled the thing
That couldn't be done, and he did it!
Somebody scoffed: "Oh, you'll never do that;
At least no one ever has done it;"
But he took off his coat and he took off his hat
And the first thing we knew he'd begun it.
With a lift of his chin and a bit of a grin,
Without any doubting or quiddit,
He started to sing as he tackled the thing
That couldn't be done, and he did it.
There are thousands to tell you it cannot be done,
There are thousands to prophesy failure,
There are thousands to point out to you one by one,
The dangers that wait to assail you.
But just buckle in with a bit of a grin,
Just take off your coat and go to it;
Just start in to sing as you tackle the thing
That "cannot be done," and you'll do it.

Edgar Albert Guest

11.

Connecting to your community

> "The need for connection and community is primal, as fundamental as the need for air, water and food."
>
> Dean Ormish, president and founder, Preventative Medicine Research Institute, California

Everyone wants to belong. From the wisdom of Desmond Tutu's *ubuntu* we know "a person is a person through other persons". Without others around us we'd never learn to speak. If you've had fun making faces at a gurgling baby you know you've connected and there's real communication. Psychologists identify connection as crucial to developing the social skills we need to get by as adults. Health professionals know it's crucial to staying well at any age.

I'm not the only one concerned we're losing this.

ChatGPT is not a real friend. Pacifying your toddler with a video is light years away from reading or chatting to them. Swiping out at the checkout creates zero connection with store staff. And increasingly we live in high-rise isolation with loneliness unsurprisingly on the up. Long-term loneliness is bad news, as bad for us as fifteen cigarettes a day according to the US surgeon general, causing depression and putting us at greater risk of dementia and more... but I will stop there.[27]

27 The impact of loneliness: www.hhs.gov/sites/default/files/surgeon-general-social-connection-advisory.pdf

So this is a call to play your part in making sure the communities you're part of positively thrive.

How about starting with a spider diagram? The areas of your life and the people there you should perhaps pay more attention to:

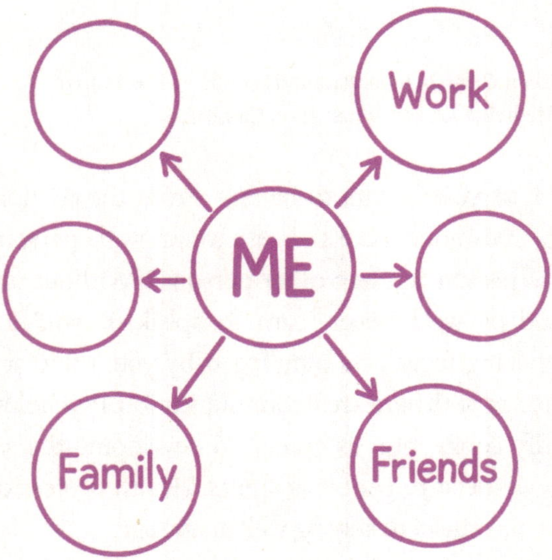

When you think about it you're probably connected to a whole host of different groups on a regular basis. Beyond family, friends and work colleagues, think about school, neighbours, gym, choir, book club, sports, the other regulars at the pub or your place of worship. Anyone walking a dog knows that when dogs want to get together conversations with those holding the leads soon follow. It took Covid for the street where I live to create a WhatsApp group. We swap babysitters, welcome newcomers, recommend electricians and plumbers as well as – inevitably – taking in each other's deliveries and warning each other when the parking's been suspended.

If you're brave enough you could take a leaf out of the book of a young couple who, having moved into their first home, invited everyone in the street to come round to an open-house evening. Room tidied, drinks, glasses, nibbles out, they waited. Would anyone turn up? About 45 minutes after the stated arrival time, the doorbell rang and within a few minutes the party was in full swing.

For anyone less able to get out and about, Age UK runs both a Telephone Friendship Service, matching people with volunteer friends to chat for an hour a week, and Silverline: a 24/7 chance to chat.[28] You don't need a reason – you can call at three in the morning if you need to. A friendly voice when you may not have had anyone to chat to for a while. Everyone feels less alone.

Part of my philosophy and the advice I give

28 Age UK telephone friendship service: www.ageuk.org.uk/services/befriending-services/sign-up-for-telephone-befriending/; Age UK Silverline helpline: www.ageuk.org.uk/services/silverline

to people going through a tough time, building businesses or dealing with any stressful challenge is "get a team around you". It's easier when you're not alone. At Whizz-Kidz we created a Kidz Board. How on earth could we hope to make the best decisions for the children we were helping if we didn't listen to them and give them a platform to come together and tell us? Connecting as a group empowered the kids and the charity was fuelled by their insights.

At another level, finding 'your tribe' is an incredibly effective medicine. Many of us feel emotionally stressed out, which in turn triggers our 'fight or flight' mode, which wears down the body, weakens immunity and accelerates biological ageing. But just as emotional stress can harm, emotional connection has the power to heal.

You may have heard about the rise in 'social prescribing'. Dr Linda Mizun, working with a team of NHS doctors and public health experts, has taken this to another level with the Hero of Health neighbourhood programme.[29] Through the Hero of Health app, people connect to their neighbours, local activities and on-demand programmes to help manage and reverse their symptoms. You're signed up by your local GP and the app connects you with others locally who want to improve their health: walking together, encouraging and supporting each other, as well as being a platform with lots of advice on diet, sleep and more. It's an innovative, fun, neighbourhood-driven model that meets people where they are and is already

29 Hero of Health: www.heroofhealth.com

having amazingly positive results. GP visits are down by an incredible 44%. For every 400 people who sign up the NHS saves an estimated £600,000. There's a 78% reported reduction in anxiety and depression. Fewer heart attacks and strokes as people connect and 'something powerful happens'. Community encouragement and support help people get better.

David's story is a great example.

David's story

"I was spiralling, four stone overweight, on anti-depressants, my type 2 diabetes getting worse. Signed off work with stress, I felt invisible. I loved my job in mental health, but couldn't feel its impact anymore. I felt isolated, exhausted, and losing hope.

Then my GP referred me to a local neighbourhood's lifestyle and social activity app which began to change everything.

I started with small steps: joining local walks, meeting neighbours and sharing honest conversations. But through those moments, something powerful happened— I found my people. My tribe. And with them came purpose.

Surrounded by a supportive, empowered community, I lost weight, came off antidepressants and reversed my diabetes.

Today, I'm a facilitator for the Hero of

Health app that helped turn my life around. I work to inspire my neighbours to take back control of their health just like me.

If I hadn't reached rock bottom, I'd never have found this version of myself. The app gave me the people, the tools and the belief to turn my life around. Now I wake up every day ready to help others do the same. That's everything."

Let's celebrate an NHS team helping people make themselves better, not with just another prescription! And wish her team good luck as they plan to expand the programme nationwide. Until it lands near you, Dr Mizun has a couple of tips: smile when you make eye contact with anyone and if you're feeling in need of a hug and there's no one near, try hugging yourself – both will boost your oxytocin levels and you'll feel better!

Proof that connection isn't just good for the soul, it's powerful medicine for the body.

Peer support works in multiple environments. When you've been through something yourself you can share the experience and knowledge you've gained along the way, offering encouragement and support.

The Loss Foundation

Dr Erin Hope Thompson, founder and CEO of The Loss Foundation has some thoughts on this:[30]

"Why did I set up The Loss Foundation? So many people get cancer and there are lots of charities, but when someone dies as my dad did, there's a real silence. There was a moment when I realised my stepmum had lost her soulmate. 'I just want to speak to someone who understands.' Surely there must be a cancer specific bereavement service? There wasn't.

It's not rocket science, bringing people together who can talk about how hard this is. I continue to be wowed by it. It's incredibly transformative. When someone dies lots of people flood round and then... silence comes in.

Many people find us because it's 11 pm, they can't sleep and they google. Anywhere between two weeks to 25 years down the line. Some people don't need this, but for those that do and don't get support the need never goes away. Peer support isn't therapy, it's empathy shared, strength multiplied. One of the biggest risks is social isolation in grief. Getting together with others in the same boat prevents that social isolation, depression and anxiety. At a fraction of the cost of NHS support. It's powerful and it works.

30 The Loss Foundation: www.theloss foundation.org

Recently a lady who'd lost her husband to cancer six years ago came to an in-person event. Her two children were very young at the time so she'd no space to find what she needed. The group was the first time she'd spoken about her grief. She came away feeling totally validated, normalised; just speaking to other husbands and wives was a powerful breath of fresh air. She didn't know others had similar thoughts. She'd held everything to herself. Like so many others who come in anxious it was transformative for her. There were hugs, smiles and she left laughing."

Anything you're going through is better in a community of others who really understand. On a lighter note, shared baby advice, gardening tips and recipes help make the world go round. Nothing is too small. Sharing gets an A+ in my book!

In our ever more complex world I'm encouraged by the rise in Citizens' Assemblies.[31] A random representative group of people is recruited, briefed on a topic, deliberates, comes to a decision by secret ballot and reports to policy-makers. My instinct is that not being got at by self-interested lobbyists is one reason for their success. Assemblies think through complex issues without public protests or political resignations for having voted 'the wrong way'. One of the most high-profile examples was in Ireland, where the laws

31 Information on setting up Citizens' Assemblies: sharedfuturecic.org.uk

on the highly emotive issues of same sex marriage and abortion were changed with input from Citizens' Assemblies. In England, Assemblies have debated solutions for social care and reaching net zero by 2050. We need to pay attention and have more of them because, simply put, coming together and caring for each other works.

In a way everything I've written about is about caring for each other, being less ego driven, rejecting FOMO and focusing a little more on nurturing the people whose paths cross yours. Spend time and energy keeping in touch. A community doesn't need to be big; it just needs to involve honest and open support of its members. So this is a call to find your tribes and nurture them!

12.

Our camino: walk your path

"You will find that the mere resolve not to be useless, the honest desire to help other people, will, in the quickest and most delicate of ways, improve yourself. "

John Ruskin

In June 2024, my wife Shuna and I walked the Camino Portuguese – from Porto in Portugal to Santiago de Compostela in Galicia, northern Spain. A mere 140 miles in eleven days!

The Camino is a network of over 281 paths, encompassing more than 51,500 miles of routes through 29 different European countries.

These pilgrimage routes and paths all finish in the main Cathedral Square in Santiago. People come from all over the world to walk the Caminos, of all faiths and none, of all ages including solo travellers, families with their children and babies in slings, fathers and sons, mothers and daughters, groups of friends and chosen family – all walking for different reasons. Most walk to find space in their lives, the time to think and consider their own paths, and yes, some to do a traditional Christian pilgrimage. Through wonderful countryside, by the side of streams and rivers, farms, through hamlets, villages and lovely small towns.

As you pass other pilgrims everyone greets each other with "Buen Camino" which literally translated is Spanish for 'good road'. It can also mean good path or good way, the path being both physical and spiritual. It is the greeting shared by pilgrims, hikers and cyclists on the Camino and also by local people who wish you well.

In my experience and the experience of very many others, you start your walk with the day and the next destination planned in the forefront of your mind, almost like normal life.

But after only a few days the Camino takes over.

‘Walker, there is no path. The path makes itself as you walk”

In the original Spanish: “Caminante, no hay Camino, se hace camino al andar”

One day I was on my own, quietly sipping a beer in a café by the mediaeval bridge in Ponte de Lima, a lovely small town in Portugal. I was watching the locals bustle about to get ready and prepare for the following day's fiesta, which involved a bull being paraded through the town and then killed.

As my thoughts wandered and I watched and listened to everyone around me busily preparing for the event, I had an 'aha' moment.

Which, simply put, was that all the ideas and thoughts in this short book – which I have written for an English-speaking audience because that's the language I speak in and also think in – must apply to them too!

Insecurity, worries about their relationships, love lives, work, finances, health – all are universal.

It is not just me, or you, or everyone we know, who are insecure and face bumps in our lives. Everyone is and does. Thus, the need to care for each other and to come alongside others having a difficult time – to help other people – is an international one. The national boundaries we've erected and fought over century after century can only be broken down by kindness, compassion and generosity.

We must all resolve to join with others and become better humans.

"Buen Camino."

Your action list

I'm assuming you're busy and don't think you need more to do. So this is a quick reference list of things that ask you perhaps to think differently, rather than take up too much time. Just start with a couple and have fun. In the words of Edgar Albert Guest:

> "Just buckle in with a bit of a grin
> Just take off your coat and go to it."

1. If you only do one thing today, show up and let someone know they're loved. Just smiling at passers-by will boost your oxytocin!
2. Who do you know who's going through a rough patch right now? Get in touch.
3. When serendipity happens – anything you come across, any random conversation or meeting that seems by chance but sparks your interest – follow up. Even when we don't know what we're doing, small actions can create a wonderful ripple effect. Enjoy the journey and start today.

4. Spend a little time thinking about the few people you feel really close to. You'll know their worries, so be there for them.
5. "What are my deepest and most profound responsibilities?" Don't rush this one, but try to work it out and when you have, let it direct your life (wisdom from Mac Macartney).
6. Who in my family should I check in with to make sure they're OK? Just do it!
7. Am I holding my life back because of a long-standing issue with someone I've not forgiven? Lighten your load and work out how to do it.
8. Work out who you'd turn to with absolute confidence in extremis and make sure you keep in touch.
9. If there's anyone you could help by 'sitting in the mud' with them, go and do it. Focus on empathy. Don't minimise it. (See Simon Sinek's words in Chapter 5.)
10. Life's too short to put up with a ghastly job. Plan your escape. (Do the exercise on p.64.)
11. Whenever you can 'make a difference to that one', go for it. (The Starfish story, Chapter 7.)
12. When you look for and find a pied piper – someone changing a little bit of the world, however small – learn from them and even become one of them yourself.
13. Always follow the Golden Rule. Treat everyone as you would like to be treated.

14. Think long and hard about success and significance. What you do for yourself will die with you; it is what you do for others that will be remembered.
15. Remember the Camino saying, "Walker there is no path. The path makes itself as you walk." If you can walk the Camino I'm sure you'll find it transformative in unexpected ways. If not start making your own path. (p.117)

And an extra mission: find and follow John Sweeney! He's a wonderful human being! (p.92)

“It is the people who no one imagined anything of who do the things no one can imagine”

Attributed to Alan Turing

Acknowledgements

To my friends and first readers, thank you all for your enthusiasm, encouragement – and ideas to make *How to Be a Better Human* better: Stephen Colegrave, Marcus Exall, Sophie Taylor, Lucy Cleland, Rory Sutherland, Tim Smit, Oli Barrett, Vince Gwilliam, Richard Brass, Anya Claxton, Omar Habbal, John Sweeney, Ankur Kamalia, AJ Leon, Annabel and Will, Rebecca Skippage, Kelly and Richard Tyler, Jamie Kelsey.

To you all whose stories have been included, for the shared wisdom they bring: Dr Gabrielle Walker, Dr Fred Mulder, Mac Macartney, Terry Pulling, Mark Williamson, Jaime Thurston, Pam Warhurst, Lavinia Thomas Buhagiar, Kim Polman, Dr Linda Mizun, Dr Erin Hope Thompson.

Kyle Taylor – every writer needs a great, questioning, lucid editor. Kyle has been good to me! Plus Ella Baddeley and the Byline team.

Friends who left their wisdom with me: Prof Ricky Richardson, Archbishop Desmond Tutu, Charles Handy.

About the Author

Mike was the almost accidental co-founder and then CEO of the children's charity Whizz-Kidz, which has raised over £150 million to provide mobility equipment for more than 26,000 disabled children and young people in the UK, while directly supporting more than 48,000 young wheelchair users to live the best possible life.

Mike also co-created, with and for Weatherbys Private Bank, a series of highly successful conferences focusing on the future world we wish to see: Creating the Future.

Today Mike and his wife Shuna are partners in Our Generous Gene, encouraging individuals, families and companies to support inspirational NGOs and social enterprises making a positive difference in the UK and globally, introducing them to sources of expertise, knowledge, contacts and funds. He loves being able to help others, especially those having a challenging time. Quietly.

A favourite quote:

"It is amazing what you can accomplish if you do not care who gets the credit"

Harry S Truman